Understanding the Cultures
of the Middle East

Art, Technology, and Language across the Middle East

Greg Baldino

Cavendish
Square
New York

Published in 2017 by Cavendish Square Publishing, LLC
243 5th Avenue, Suite 136, New York, NY 10016

Library of Congress Cataloging-in-Publication Data

Names: Baldino, Greg, author.
Title: Art, technology, and language across the Middle East / Greg Baldino.
Description: New York : Cavendish Square Publishing, 2017. | Series: Understanding the cultures of the Middle East | Includes bibliographical references and index.
Identifiers: LCCN 2016029420 (print) | LCCN 2016031893 (ebook) |
ISBN 9781502623614 (library bound) | ISBN 9781502623621 (E-book)
Subjects: LCSH: Middle East--Civilization. | Art--Middle East. | Technology--Middle East. | Arabic language--Middle East. | Middle East--Languages.
Classification: LCC DS57 .B284 2017 (print) | LCC DS57 (ebook) | DDC 956--dc23
LC record available at https://lccn.loc.gov/2016029420

Editorial Director: David McNamara
Editor: Elizabeth Schmermund
Copy Editor: Rebecca Rohan
Associate Art Director: Amy Greenan
Designer: Alan Sliwinski
Production Coordinator: Karol Szymczuk
Photo Research: J8 Media

Contents

A calligrapher uses a brush and ink to write in Arabic, the same tools that have been used for centuries.

Introduction

What *is* the Middle East? In some ways, it's a name that makes almost no sense. There is no actual area called the Middle East on any official map, and the area usually called that overlaps Asia and Africa. In certain historical contexts, it sometimes includes Turkey, which is geographically also part of Europe. The name itself came into use by Western Europeans as a way to distinguish it from what was considered the "Far East"— meaning China, India, and other Southeast Asian countries. However, to the Chinese, Indians, and other East Asians, the region is

to the west, and for much of the African continent, it is north. For someone living in Seattle, Washington, the "Far East" becomes the "Near West." And for someone living in the city of Jerusalem, the "Middle East" is "here."

For this book, the Middle East will be defined as the regions of the Levant, the Gulf, and North Africa. To understand how the many nations and cultures of this area can be grouped together, we have to look at the one thing that has shaped and connected them more than anything else: the Arabic language.

All of language begins with the spoken word. Language spread verbally through the region because of **nomadic people**, who had to move from one location to another in pursuit of fresh water and edible plants for both foraging and feeding their livestock. The written characters used in Arabic are believed to have come from the Nabateans, who lived in what is now Jordan around the beginning of the current era.

The Arabic language is complex to learn. It is written in a compressed system, where all of the letters in a word are not always written out, so knowing only the characters won't help you to read texts if you are not familiar with the whole words. It's also difficult to translate phonetically into Roman letters, as there are many sounds in Arabic pronunciations that can't be conveyed with European spellings. The United States government has classified Arabic as the second-hardest language for English speakers to learn, second only to Chinese.

What enabled Arabic to spread as far as it did has to do with the religion of Islam. In the Islamic faith, it is believed that God, called Allah in Arabic, delivered a message of prophecy to a man

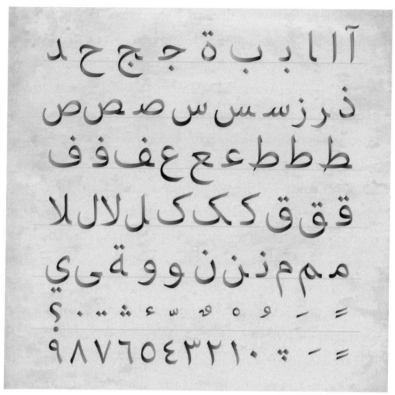

Arabic characters evolved to be easy to remember and write down.

named Muhammad. This spoken message was eventually written down as the Quran, the holy text of the Muslims. Because it was believed to come directly from Allah to Muhammad, the text was written in the **dialect** of Arabic from Muhammad's home in Mecca.

Like Christianity, Islam was an evangelical religion, meaning that people from outside the faith could convert and join. During the Arabic Conquests of the seventh century, Muslims conquered new lands and converted these people to Islam—just as Christians had done in previous centuries after their religion became the

official faith of the Roman **Empire**. For people to convert to Islam, they needed to be able to read the Quran. Translations of the text were not considered legitimate, so the Muslims taught these conquered people Arabic. While the religious language had to remain the same, the spoken Arabic would often absorb words, phrases, and pronunciations from the local dialects over time.

The two influences of Arabic and Islam had an enormous effect on the arts and sciences in the Middle East. Poetry and literature that developed in Arabic could not have happened in any other language, as the way it is written on the page allows for repetitions and forms that can become clunky and awkward when translated into another language. The Islamic religion discourages against art depicting people or animals who are or were alive, so the calligraphic style of Arabic came to be recognized as a form of visual art unto itself. As a language, it has proven to be very useful for exploring and explaining scientific and mathematical ideas, and the poetic nature of Arabic made it possible for whole books to be easily memorized in the time before mechanized printing was readily available.

Today, almost three million people in the world speak Arabic as their first language. Of the many countries this book will discuss, only two do not have Arabic as their primary language: Israel, where **Hebrew** is the official language, and Iran, which uses the Persian language of **Farsi**. However, even in these countries, many people will still have some fluency in Arabic. Unfortunately, in America, Arabic has become a controversial language. Following the terrorist attacks on September 11, 2001, Islamophobia and the fear of Muslims has become more rampant, and many people

reading books on airplanes have been removed at the request of fearful passengers who cannot separate Arabic from Islam and Islam from violence. At the time of the writing of this book, an Italian mathematician—whose skin tone and hair texture is shared by many people on both sides of the Mediterranean Sea—was removed from a flight and questioned because an American woman saw his advanced math calculations and thought he was writing in Arabic.

The goal of this book is to explore the many contributions to art and science that have been made by people of this region. There is a profound wealth of creative work that has come out of the Middle East, both in the past and in the present, as well as vital technological discoveries that continue to transform the world today. All of this has been made possible by language, a technology—and an art form—with the incredible power to connect people.

New technology and traditional culture are both part
of life in modern Iran.

1

The History of Art, Technology, and Language across the Middle East

M any historians believe that the area that today comprises Iraq, Syria, Iran, and Kuwait, was the site of the first human civilization. Eventually called Mesopotamia by the ancient Greeks, which means "between two rivers," the region is framed by the Tigris and Euphrates rivers. Nourished by the fertile land between these two rivers, humans migrated from this area throughout the world over thousands and thousands of years. The Middle East, then,

is the foundational site of human culture, which begins before anything else with language.

Speak and Be Spoken To

All languages begin as spoken communication. We can't know exactly what the first languages sounded like because languages are always changing, and it is difficult to trace a particular language back several millennia. But the earliest forms of speech would have been integral to the survival of early humans and the development of civilization. Words developed according to the needs and environments of early people; for example, a tribe living near only a freshwater river would only have one word for water, while one that was also near the sea would have words for freshwater and salty sea water. A language that is specific to a particular group or region is called a dialect.

Nomadic people, like these Omani Bedouin, have been a part of Middle Eastern culture since before recorded history.

Language doesn't grow without new ideas and terms being added to it. In the ancient world, there were two ways for new words to come into a culture. One way was via nomadic communities. Nomads were people who didn't live in one permanent location. They traveled around from place to place with all their belongings, usually looking for food and water. They would often set up a camp for a month or so, allowing their animals to graze, before moving on. Another way different forms of speech moved around was through traders. As a civilization began to develop, some people made a business of taking goods such as crops and crafts to other places that had a need for them.

Nomads and traders had to learn new languages as they moved around. For the nomads, it was important to be able to communicate that they were not hostile, and how long they might be staying. Traders needed to be able to negotiate with their customers, to understand what things people needed and how much they were willing to trade for them. What happened in many cases is that a type of combined language, called pidgin, was constructed. Pidgin means a form of a language with a simple grammar and words borrowed from two or more different cultures. **Pidgin languages** appear all over the world when people of different languages need to communicate. Words from one group will sometimes become part of another over time through pidgin dialects. Because of extensive trading across the Mediterranean Sea, for example, Greek, Latin, and Arabic influenced each other, modifying the spelling and pronunciation of words to fit into their own dialect and alphabet.

Writing It Down to Remember It Later

As human civilization developed, language took a new form: the written word. Before writing was invented, the earliest markings for communication were simplified pictures. These pictographs first emerged in ancient Sumerian culture, located in modern-day Iraq, around 3300 BCE. The earliest alphabets took their characters from simplified pictures that came to represent words, so instead of a drawing of a cow, for example, a person in ancient Egypt would make a simple picture of a cow's head. Over hundreds of years, this simple picture became a mark that could be made with a few quick strokes of a writing utensil and eventually became the letter Aleph in Arabic and the A in the Roman alphabet. How written languages developed had a lot to do with what was used for recording the marks. Writing that was done on stone or in clay had to be very simple, because the material was difficult to make marks in. Some cultures, such as the ancient Egyptians, were able to make an early form of paper called papyrus, made using the papyrus plant, which could be written on using ink. Marks made using tools that left a mark on the surface instead of in the material could be more elaborate and artistic.

Written language had three major uses that changed civilization and sped up the development of human technology and culture. First, it allowed for written records, which made large-scale business transactions possible. Using written language, two merchants could record that they agreed to trade one person's cows for a cart of another person's pottery. Eventually, this kind of record would evolve into money. It also meant that formal histories

In Dubai, this library helps preserve information and culture to make it available to everyone.

could be written. Whereas before the only record of events was through oral storytelling, a written language meant that history could be more permanently recorded. When you hear the phrase "before recorded history" in a book, that refers to a time where there were no written records to survive for present-day historians to understand (before the fourth century BCE). Possibly the most important application of writing, however, was that it made information accessible to many people. It meant that people didn't have to start learning a new subject from scratch if they could get ahold of a book someone else had made.

For a long time, writing had to be done by hand, first with a stylus, or an object with a hard point, and later with a pen. This made long written works extremely time-consuming, rare, and, therefore, expensive. One person could spend much of their entire life writing a single book, which would then be kept in a private collection, mosque, or the library of a school. Only the very wealthy could afford to own books, so people like doctors had to memorize entire volumes of medical knowledge. When the printing press first came to the Persian Empire in the sixteenth century from China, it made books available to many people and, most importantly, allowed books to be transported to other places, thus bringing new ideas to people.

Higher, Further, Faster, More

Many years later, in 1837, the telegraph, a machine that could communicate over long distances with a code of short and long electrical signals, was invented. It came to the Ottoman Empire in 1855. Over the next fifty years, telegraph cable was laid between major cities, creating a network of communication that opened up the different countries to each other and to the outside world.

This new invention helped to centralize regional governments, which some of the nomadic **Bedouins** found intrusive to their way of life. The telegraph was a unifying force economically and politically by reducing communication time across the Middle East. Government administration was different in places that had the telegraph and those that didn't; where without the telegraph it took days for dispatches to arrive, news and orders could be

sent instantaneously with the new technology. The telegraph later paved the way for the telephone, which further opened up communication, as it didn't require an operator who knew Morse code to send and receive messages.

It wasn't until the 1920s that broadcast radio began to make its way into the Middle East. After World War II, national radio stations became a government priority, and the number of receivers started to increase dramatically. By the late seventies, over twenty million households in the region had one or more home radios. The popularity of radio was due, in part, to the low cost of receivers and the ability to use batteries to power them—important because many rural villagerss, nomadic groups, and even some city dwellers didn't have electricity in their homes.

Although more conservative countries resisted the transition to broadcasting, they soon realized that transmissions from other nations couldn't be blocked out from their own people, and their radio silence would thus turn up the volume on outside cultures and politics. Television took longer to catch on because TV sets were more expensive and scarce, just as books had been thousands of years earlier.

The internet and cellular phones changed communication even further, and with smartphones, it's now affordable for people to have access to worldwide information and culture from their pockets. Whereas once doctors had to memorize whole books of medical knowledge, today an ordinary person can check the side effects of a medication with a few taps on a screen, and travelers to an unfamiliar culture can download an app to learn the local language and customs while their plane flies across the world.

Art as Communication

Historically, written and spoken language hasn't been the only form of communication in the Middle East. Artistic mediums such as music, theater, poetry, and visual arts have all been used to convey complex personal and cultural ideas. While there are many languages that fell out of use before they could be documented, a lot of physical artworks from thousands of years ago have survived. Even some performative art has survived, either by being passed along through families and communities, or by becoming incorporated into other works and traditions.

The first forms of artwork would have been made as part of everyday life. Much of what comprises folk art is produced to be practical; it was rare for such works to be purely decorative. This was especially true for the nomadic people, who couldn't afford to carry anything with them that wasn't essential to their survival. Even people living in small villages or early cities wouldn't have had the time or resources to make something that didn't also serve a practical purpose. Many early artworks were things like pottery that could store water or be used to cook, or **fiber arts** such as blankets, rugs, and clothing. The colors and patterns chosen would have important significance; the marks on a cooking pot could contain a family history, and the different dyes on a headdress could signify an important event.

While a lot of folk art would be made by an individual or kept within a family, the performing arts were all about community. Songs, dances, and storytelling all needed two things: performers and an audience. Sometimes the two would become one, and

Textile art, like the Bedouin blankets draped on these dromedaries, is both practical and decorative.

everyone would join in singing and dancing together. These arts were important because they helped to create a communal identity that existed beyond just living close together. Storytelling and theater also functioned as a form of journalism in the cities, and allowed performers to reenact and comment on major events soon after they happened. The performing arts functioned in many ways like the internet does today: as a way to connect with friends and find out the latest news.

The more that individuals and communities practiced these arts, the better they became, and soon standards of art were formalized. This had two effects that have carried over to today. One is that it became a form of cultural preservation. Artwork that has survived tells us a lot about a culture and where their creators came from. If we look at markings on a water jug in Morocco and match them with a pattern on a blanket from Libya, we can infer that there was some contact between these cultures. The other effect of formalizing art is that it began a profession; art became something that, if a person was good enough, they could create works to sell instead of gathering food or irrigating crops.

Once there were people who were noticeably more skilled at an art form than other people, they became in demand. In smaller communities, where most people were at the same level economically, this didn't matter as much. However, in the cities, where there were wealthier classes of merchants and aristocrats, artists could find themselves hired to produce art for one person or family. It was worth it for these artists to not only be very good, but to develop a recognizable style, almost like a brand identity.

For the people who had a lot of wealth, art didn't have to be practical—it could be purely ornate. People wanted beautiful art to show off to others, like elaborate jewelry made with precious metals and gems, or large sculptures that would take a long time to produce and require a lot of resources to make, as well as a space to show it off in. These works of art existed to be as much a display of the status of an individual or family as they did as a pure expression of aesthetic beauty. This was important because it allowed art forms to develop that otherwise wouldn't have been

able to develop as a folk art; Persian poetry, for example, came into being almost entirely thanks to the systems of patronage.

Although they technically weren't of the wealthy class, religious groups would also commission artisans. Sometimes people from the upper classes would provide the money for artists to do work on behalf of a temple or church, and on other occasions they would work free of charge as a gesture of faith. When Islam became a major religion in the medieval era, religious art became

Geometric designs, like these found in the tomb of the Persian poet Hafez, are common in Islamic art.

a whole new field, as the Muslim faith proscribes against depicting living beings. Whereas an artist commissioned by the Catholic Church could decorate a chapel with images of biblical figures, an Islamic artist couldn't create such depictions. Geometric designs then became very popular in everything from architecture to fabric patterns.

Art for the people and art for the elite came together in the twentieth century as technology and art came together to create the mass media of recording and broadcasting. Making movies and television shows are too costly to be only for a small group of people, no matter how rich they are, but the common people couldn't afford to make it on their own. One person with no props or even a costume beyond their clothes could perform theater in the street, but recording the same performance required people to operate the camera, record the sound, light the set, and more.

Recording these performances wasn't enough—it needed to be accessible to people. Once a movie had been recorded, it needed a theater to show it in with a projector and sound system. A television show required even more: it wasn't enough to record it and broadcast it, people needed a television set in order to watch it. Mass media became an art form that only worked if wealthy people invested to make it available to as many people as possible.

Language, Art, and Technology

Language and art both influence, and are influenced by, developing technology. What technology actually is can be explored in many different ways. It can be viewed as physically applied science and

mathematics, taking abstract ideas and deriving a concrete effect from them. Another way to look at it is as an art form that is guided toward practicality and clarity rather than aesthetic beauty. We can even describe technology as its own language; as a reader's attention follows a sentence to understanding, so too does an electrical charge follow a circuit to completion.

Throughout this book, language, technology, and art will in many ways blur together. All three of them move us together from the past to the present and into the future. To explore these three aspects of Middle Eastern culture, we must answer the following three questions, although not always in the same order.

What Do We Have?

An artist has to work with the materials that are available to them and that, in turn, becomes part of their style. If there are plants or minerals nearby with strong colors, these may be made into dyes or paints. Soil with lots of clay can be used to make pottery, sculptures, or beads. Tall grasses growing in abundance by a riverbank can be used to make baskets. Resources don't just mean physical things, either; a village that has a lot of musicians offers a lot of learning experiences, either by direct instruction or just by observing and enjoying their work.

Today, a scientist working on a project can order supplies from anywhere in the world: a doctor researching medicine for new cures will need access to lots of different plants, which may not all grow nearby. Experiments with precious or rare metals, such as natural magnets and mercury, might require larger amounts of supplies than can be found in one region alone. Lenses and prisms

of particular sizes and shapes may need to be brought in from glassblowers in other cities. However, up until a few centuries ago, technology was dependent on what resources were close by. Cities were important to technological development because they were almost always built on trade routes. The development of technology in the Middle East was aided by its position between the markets and shipping routes of Europe and Asia, but that doesn't mean it didn't have influence of its own. The materials and equipment that were available to local scientists allowed them to develop unique scientific insights, and they were often able to use that knowledge to expand on the ideas of other cultures in unforeseen directions.

What Do We Need?

Both art and technology work to answer needs. Art tells us who we are and who we could be. It makes sense of life and the human condition. It takes our fears and our passions and gives us a way to understand them and have some control over them. Technology moves our survival concerns from the animal to the human. It means having enough food to not have to constantly hunt for the next meal. It creates light in darkness, and can make a hostile environment something that can be endured.

What Does This Change?

Technology reduces work, and that makes more space and time for art. But technology also creates new needs to take care of the old ones. Today, a refrigerator can keep foods fresh and accessible for days, weeks, and even months longer than we could preserve

food a thousand years ago; but to do so it needs a steady intake of electrical energy. Art gives us answers, but often in the form of a new question. If a song or a painting can give us a better idea of who we are and what we want, then we shift and change. The questions then shift too: Who are we now? What do we want now?

And language changes along with all of this. Language is an artistic technology and a technological art, both an end product and a catalyzing agent. And it is constantly evolving, spurring on both our development and adapting to our own changes.

Art, language, and technology are the foundation stones of humanity.

The ruins of the Tachara date back to the beginnings of the Persian Empire in Persepolis.

2

Art, Technology, and Language in the Gulf Region

Surrounded by the waters of the Red Sea, the Arabian Sea, and the Persian Gulf, the lands of the Arabian Peninsula are known as the Gulf Region. For most of its history, the area was primarily home to wandering nomadic groups. Because the region is dominated by the Arabian Desert, it was never sought and fought for by European powers like the Mediterranean regions. That changed in the mid-twentieth century when oil prospectors found major reserves of oil beneath the sands. Suddenly, poor regions

became wealthy nations, and the rest of the world stood up and took notice. Today, these countries work to both preserve their heritage and shape an international future.

Bahrain

The nation of Bahrain is an archipelago of many small islands off the coast of Saudi Arabia. One of the first countries to convert to Islam and the first in the Middle East to adapt to an oil economy, the desert islands were also early to utilize the internet in 1995. Today, political unrest against the government is largely enabled by the use of social media sites to communicate and locate information, as the news outlets in the country are heavily biased.

Along with Kuwait, Bahrain was a major center for the growth of Arabic theater in the Gulf Region. Amateur dramatic productions became popular after World War II, which led to a growing number of Bahrainian playwrights and theater companies over the next few decades. In the 1970s, a move to support local playwrights and dramatists began, but it was not without certain constraints; the government was quick to censor works that it considered to be of a political agenda, and artists sometimes found their works under suspicion for perceived subtexts in their plays.

Iran

The Persian Empire was one of the longest consistent cultures in the Middle East. Its influence in science, philosophy, politics, and art has been a part of the entire region's history. Today, the empire is gone; its culture and language, Farsi, are contained within the

modern-day borders of the country of Iran. Its influence on Arabic literature, however, is enormous.

The Business of Wine and Verse

In the Persian city of Shiraz, merchants from Spain and Greece would come to buy and barter for fabrics and spices from India and other Asian countries. The merchants of Shiraz became very wealthy from these markets, as well as from their own product: wine.

An alcoholic beverage made from grapes that have been allowed to ferment, wine was popular in the ancient world both for its flavor and also because the process of making it killed bacteria, making it safer to drink than river water. Grapes would be collected and crushed, then mixed with sugar to allow chemical reactions to transform it. The wines of Shiraz were very popular because of the quality of their grapes, and archeologists have found that Shirazis were the earliest known people to have a scientific system for producing it.

Shiraz is located on a grassy plain next to mountains. Standing more than 5,000 feet (1,524 meters) above sea level, this region's mild and comfortable climate is ideal for growing grapes, as well as other fruits and vegetables. With their food needs taken care of and a popular wine that brought in more money from outside than it cost to make it, the merchants and winemakers of Shiraz became very wealthy. What did they do with all that extra money? They bought art!

These rich Shirazis paid artists to make art especially for them. One of the most popular forms of art they commissioned was

poetry about themselves. These poems would be recited aloud in the courts of the rich and powerful, and this form became known as the **ghazal**. Many of these powerful families were interested in a mystical form of the Islamic religion called **Sufism**, and several major poets from medieval Persia were Sufis. Many ghazals were written to be read as metaphors, so a poem about the relationship between a courtier and his prince could also be taken as being about a mortal and God. For a very long time, this kind of Persian poetry was viewed as an integral part of Iranian culture.

In 1979, Iran's culture standards shifted when Ayatollah Khomeini took control of the country, transforming it into an Islamic state. Following the revolution, academic institutions in Iran were shut down for three years while intellectuals with strong Western influences seen to be in conflict with Islamic ideology were removed. The purge was finally completed with a large number of books and articles being banned by the government. Iran's progress as a modern culture had been reversed. As a form of artistic protest, many Iranian writers returned to the ghazal. The combination of flexibility and formality was compatible with modern free-verse poetic styles, and gave a way to address the government's violation of human rights while asserting a cultural identity over a national one.

One of the most important contemporary writers in Iran is Shahrnush Parsipur, who was first published as a teenager. For her work, which has largely focused on the lives of women in modern-day Iran, she has been arrested and incarcerated several times, and her works have been banned by the government. After leaving the country in 1994, she wrote in her memoir that in Iran

Rumi

Rumi was born to native Farsi-speaking parents in a part of medieval Persia that is now Afghanistan. His family had been Islamic preachers for several generations.

When the Mongol invasion reached Persia in the early twelfth century, his father, a theologian and jurist (lawyer), took the family and a group of his disciples out of their home city of Balkh. In the city of Nishapur, a chance meeting with a poet sparked Rumi's interest in writing.

Following in his family's tradition, Rumi dedicated himself to the mystical Islamic traditions of Sufism. After almost a decade of study, he came to work in law and in religious education. He also produced some of the Islamic world's greatest and most well-loved poetry.

Then, on November 15, 1244, Rumi's life was completely changed when he met a man who would become his spiritual mentor: Shams-e Tabrizi. From an accomplished teacher and jurist, Rumi renounced all outward signs of wealth and accomplishment and became an ascetic, or someone who lives very strictly and simply. On the night of December 5, 1248, as Rumi and Shams were talking, Shams was called to the back door. He went out, never to be seen again. Some scholars believe that disciplines of Rumi who were jealous of his relationship with Shams murdered him.

Rumi died on December 17, 1273, in Konya, located today in Turkey; his body was interred beside that of his father. His epitaph reads:

> When we are dead, seek not our tomb in the earth,
> but find it in the hearts of men.

"the laws were such that they turned a person into stone—silent and immobile."

Iraq

As travel between distant countries opened up, and printing slowly started to develop, ideas began to spread between thinkers thousands of miles apart. Being right in the middle of trade routes between Europe and Asia, many scholars in the Middle East began to find out about new ideas and started putting them together in radical new ways. One such scholar was al-Khwarizmi of Baghdad, who was one of the first people in the Muslim world to read Ptolemy's treatise on astronomy, *The Syntaxis Mathematica*, which had just been translated into Arabic. The book had been written almost seven hundred years earlier and was considered a revolutionary text in early astronomy. Studying also from the work of Indian mathematicians, Al-Khwarizmi learned about their ideas of decimalized mathematics, which allowed for very precise calculations. But his most important contribution to math and science was ... nothing.

At the time, the numerical systems of the world were built around groups of tens. In Europe, for example, Roman numerals were used, with letter characters like I, V, X, and others in different combinations representing amounts. To write the number twenty-four, you would write XXIV: two Xs to represent two multiples of ten, followed by IV which stands for one (I) less from five (V). Arabic and other languages used simpler systems, with individual symbols to represent one through nine and multiples of ten. But

what no one had was a number to represent nothing: zero didn't exist. The Greeks had the idea of nothing, but they didn't have anything to represent it. Meanwhile, Indian mathematicians would use a mark on the page of a stylized dot when they needed to indicate an empty sum, but this was treated as a placeholder, not an actual number. al-Khwarizmi was the first person to assign it an actual numeric symbol and treat it like an amount.

Why was this so important to al-Khwarizmi and to mathematics in general? His major work was the first book on algebra, a system of mathematics that goes beyond arithmetic to allow for calculating equations with amounts that are unknown. It's the gateway to even more advanced systems like calculus and trigonometry, which enable everything from brain surgery to rocket science. Hundreds of years later, the German philosopher Gottfried Leibniz would use the numbers zero and one to develop his system of binary notation to represent letters and characters. Alan Turing was a British mathematician tasked with breaking German codes during World War II. He used binary as the foundation of computer calculations, making it possible for pressing a key to make a letter appear on a screen in a fraction of a second.

Today, we have the internet connecting computers all around the world to bring people in different countries and cultures together to exchange ideas and communicate. All of this is because an Englishman in the mid-twentieth century had access to the ideas of a German philosopher from three hundred years earlier, which were built on the concepts of an Islamic mathematician, who had taken the ideas of two different cultures and used them to create nothing from something.

Art from the Ashes

In the aftermath of the American invasion of Iraq, a new future for the country's arts opened in 2016 when the palace of former dictator Saddam Hussein was transformed into an art museum. The first new museum opened in decades, it was created with the

A palace before the occupation of Iraq becomes an art museum after the occupation.

hopes of creating a renewed interest for art and culture in the city of Basra. The palace was turned over to the Iraqi State Board of Antiquities and Heritage, which raised over three million dollars from the civic government and a British charity for the project. The museum's collection includes almost four thousand individual objects on display in four halls dedicated to the different major eras of Iraq's history. The new museum is one of many steps being taken by the post-occupation government to both preserve the regional culture and celebrate its contemporary creativity.

Kuwait

The flat, pebble-strewn desert land of Kuwait became the setting for major international action in 1990. That was the year that Iraq, its neighbor to the north, invaded Kuwait under the leadership of then-president Saddam Hussein. Although the Iraqi forces were driven out by a coalition of United Nations militaries within a few months, the damage done was great. Kuwaiti civilians were tortured and killed, and cities suffered massive damage from bombs and missiles that destroyed buildings and roads. Geographically smaller than the state of New Jersey, Kuwait has scarce agricultural resources. There is very little soil fertile enough to grow crops, and freshwater is extremely limited. However, like other countries in the Gulf, Kuwait has important oil reserves that were largely discovered in the early- to mid-twentieth century.

Although modern art in Kuwait follows the Islamic prohibition against depictions of people and animals, it is very diverse in its styles, with little influence from traditional Islamic art. Many

paintings will use abstract shapes and swirling colors to express emotional energy. Modern art has been supported in the country since the mid-twentieth century, especially with the founding of the National Council for Culture, Arts, and Letters in 1973. The Council works to support emerging artists and art forms as well as supporting the production and preservation of traditional Kuwaiti crafts, such as weaving and leather-tooling.

Oman

Forming the southeast corner of the Arabian Peninsula, the Sultanate of Oman has an economy driven more by tourism than by its moderate reserves of oil. Throughout the year, the country hosts numerous cultural and artistic festivals, highlighting traditional Omani culture and contemporary crafts and performing arts.

One of its most recent festivals is Muscat Fashion Week, which celebrates the work of Omani designers as well as international fashions. Set in the country's capital city, the event premiered in 2011 to great international acclaim and is supported by both the monarchy and Omani aristocrats. That same year, the Sultanate also opened the Royal Opera House Muscat, a world-class performance venue that also includes a floral garden, artisan shops, and luxury restaurants. At the time of its construction, the only other European-style opera house was located in Cairo, Egypt. The complex has been host to many international performances ranging from jazz to ballet, and the growth of interest in classical music led to a new radio station to promote musical culture.

Qatar

Qatar was one of the world's largest exporters of pearls for a very long time. When the pearl market collapsed in the 1920s, many in Qatar had no idea how the country would ever recover. Food became scarce, and what little support they might have gotten from other countries dried up during the Great Depression when the American economy affected the wealth and stability of many nations, even those that were not directly involved with the United States. Then, in the late 1930s, oil prospectors came to the region and discovered that the country sat on large reserves of oil. Unfortunately, the Qatari people would have to wait over a decade to take advantage of this, as the outbreak of World War II essentially shut down international commerce. It was not until 1949 that Qatar's oil industry began, which led to a much-needed revitalization of the economy.

Unfortunately, as many Middle Eastern nations that abruptly became oil-producing economies in the twentieth century discovered, with more money comes more problems. Within the Qatari royal family, several members made demands for access to the country's new wealth. Threats were made to the **emir**, who, despite his country's sudden financial prosperity, knew he would not have the resources to handle a power struggle within his own family. The country had been a **protectorate** of the United Kingdom since 1916, but a new arrangement was made that put Qatar directly under British control. This lasted until 1971, when Qatar became fully independent.

Diversity and Technology

Because of its oil reserves and strategic location—the peninsula was instrumental during the Iraq invasion for launching and receiving ships and airplanes—Qatar has strong ties with the United States. Just outside of Doha, for example, is one of Qatar's major focuses: a massive, multischool campus known as Education City. In addition to the many local schools there, the campus also includes satellite colleges for several major American universities. This makes it possible both for Qatari students to receive an international education without leaving the country, and offers American students the opportunity to study abroad. In addition to its universities, Education City also houses many research facilities, including the Qatar Science and Technology Park and the Qatar National Research Fund.

Qatari Art

Bedouin traditions have been major influences in Qatari culture. Because of their nomadic lifestyle, moving from one location to another every few months as their animals grazed at oases, they had no interest or use for art that was purely ornamental—framed paintings and statues don't travel well by camelback. Much of their creative work included things that were either easy to transport, such as jewelry made from precious metals, or that served practical purposes. Some of the fiber arts the Bedouin make includes rugs and blankets as well as clothing and baskets. There is also a long tradition of spoken-word poetry and storytelling, which continues to this day. However, publishing is beginning to

take off in the culture, as collections of plays by both Qatari- and English-language playwrights have become increasingly popular in recent years.

The ruling and wealthy classes of Qatari have historically been interested in buying and collecting art. The Al Thanis, the ruling family of Qatar, have amassed a huge collection of Islamic art. In the art world, Qatar is known for being the world's biggest buyer of art by value.

Saudi Arabia

Until 1932, the area that is the country of Saudi Arabia today was home to wandering nomadic peoples. With the discovery of the largest reserves of oil in the world and the rise to power of the Saud family, however, the region came together as not only a kingdom but a major world power. One quarter of the world's oil comes from Saudi Arabia, which afforded the country the luxury of being able to remain isolated for most of the last century; foreigners were not allowed to visit the country until the year 2000 except for business or political purposes. As the country has been opening up, they have struggled to balance outside cultures with their traditional values and customs.

One of those customs is the *ardah*, the national dance of Saudi Arabia. When performing it, the men are arranged in two rows, each row facing the other (only men are allowed to perform the ardah). The men hold a sword in one hand and a scabbard in the other. Accompanying the dance is music played on drums and lyrical poetry performed by a male singer. Sword dances exist in

The national dance of Saudi Arabia, the *ardah*, is performed with swords.

cultures around the world, and it's believed that they originated as a show of skill by warriors. Today, sword dances like the ardah are celebratory and are more likely to be danced at weddings and festivals than before battle.

The United Arab Emirates (UAE)

Originally known for its Bedouin trade routes, the southern coast of the Persian Gulf became the United Arab Emirates in 1971. An emirate is a territory ruled by an emir, a type of monarch in

Arabic-speaking countries. The UAE is a constitutional federation, made up of seven emirates: Abu Dhabi, Dubai, Ajman, Umm al-Quwain, Ras al-Khaimah, Fujairah, and Sharjah. The flag representing the federation features a color scheme that appears on several Middle Eastern flags: red, green, white, and black. The significance of the colors comes from a thirteenth-century poem by Safi al-Dinal al-Hilli. In the poem, the colors signify the lush fertile land (green,) blood spilled by sword combat (red), the purity of the warriors (white), and the fierceness of the battle (black).

A book fair is held every year in Abu Dhabi, which celebrates and promotes the work of Emirati authors, characters, and history. Mohammed al-Murr is a prominent Emirati author who has worked to encourage his culture's literary merit. In 2015, he edited the book *Emirati Creative Works*, which collected English language translations of poems and short stories for international readers. "The UAE is now open to the trends of international literature, mainly thanks to technology," he said while speaking at the London Book Fair. "Breaking barriers and experimenting with literature is easier, as is finding, even creating, new audiences."

Yemen

The southern tip of the Arabian Peninsula is home to a wide variety of landscapes, from mountains to coral reefs. Unfortunately, the country has also experienced much conflict in its history, both with outsiders and among its own people. As a result, and because of its scarce oil reserves, it is one of the poorest countries in the Middle East.

A Yemeni man's traditional *jambiya* dagger is worn with a decorative belt.

The signature craft of Yemeni culture is the *jambiya*, a decorative dagger. Recognized by its curved blade, the dagger is worn by Yemeni men on the front of their belts. The design of both the dagger itself and its sheath is reflective of the wearer's heritage or social standing. Some jambiyas are decorated with silver handles, while the most valuable ones are considered to be those made from the horns of the African rhinoceros. The latter has been prohibited from being made in recent years, as the rhinoceros has become endangered due to excessive hunting. The belts on which the daggers are worn are also considered works of art, and will often be decorated with lavish embroidery or detailed leatherwork.

Many traditional crafts are for sale in this *souk*, or marketplace.

3

Art, Technology, and Language in the Levant Region

T he countries grouped near the southeast coast of the Mediterranean Sea are together called the Levant, from a Greco-Latin root meaning "rising." Europeans first used this term during the early Renaissance, when international trading was exploding and the region became a major crossroads for trade. Of the three main areas of the Middle East, the Levant has had the most cross-cultural influence with Europe, from antiquity to the modern day.

Egypt

From ancient times to the present day, the life source of Egypt is the River Nile. Running between the Mediterranean Sea and Ethiopia, the waters of the river made civilization possible; providing drinking water, enabling agriculture, and serving as an important trade and transportation route. "Egypt is the gift of the Nile," wrote the ancient Greek historian Herodotus.

The ancient Egyptians depended on the annual flooding of the Nile to ensure good harvests. When the banks of the river flooded, they would leave behind mineral-rich silt, which would fertilize the soil to produce healthy crops. If there wasn't enough flooding, the soil would not be enriched, and the crops would be poor. Too much, and the clay levees built to protect the buildings would be washed over, damaging buildings.

Controlling the Nile's waters was imperative in ancient times. Water wheels were used to mechanically extract water out of the river, powered by its own currents. The water could be sent then by canals to irrigate crops. When the Romans invaded Egypt in 30 BCE, they introduced aqueducts, a type of bridge built to carry water over land instead of through it.

For a long time, Egyptians tried to construct a dam to control the flooding and create a reservoir of water. In the eleventh century, **Caliph** al-Hakim commissioned the mathematics scholar al-Haytham, mostly known for his study of optics, to figure out how to build such a construct. Realizing it was not possible with the existing technologies, al-Haytham had to feign madness to escape punishment for being unable to fulfill the ruler's wishes.

The Aswan Dam realized the dreams of ancient pharaohs.

The Caliph's dream would go unfulfilled until the Aswan Dam was constructed in 1970, which has the added modern benefit of using the currents to generate hydroelectric power. Its reservoir holds 132 cubic kilometers of water and the generators produce over 10,000 gigawatt hours of electricity every year.

Showtime!

The seasonal flooding of the Nile influenced more than just Egypt's agriculture. It has also had an impact on the country's social culture. Ancient calendars were built around the crop cycle, marking times for planting and harvesting. The flooding of the Nile was celebrated annually with the Wafaa al-Nil festival, which included singing and music, dancing, and the earliest forms of theater.

Throughout its evolution, theater in Egypt was more than just entertainment. It also functioned as a news source for informing people about current events, and provided a forum for public discussion and criticism of political and religious concerns. Theater in Egypt has drawn many influences from foreign visitors and invaders, from the French Influence brought by Napoleon to traditional Indonesian shadow puppets, but its audience has always remained the heart of the art.

Israel and Palestine

It is difficult to talk about Palestine and Israel separately, as both their histories and present day situations are intricately woven together. The foundations of their conflict go back thousands of

years to when the ancient Hebrews founded the kingdom of Israel around 1000 BCE. In the first century, the Emperor Hadrian, who had grown tired of fighting Jewish resistance to the expansion and rule of the Roman Empire, decided to dismantle the entire country. Roman soldiers destroyed their temple, exiled the Jews, and outlawed their religion. The region was renamed as the Roman province Syria Palestine. For this, Jewish people thereafter would always follow his name with the curse "May his bones be crushed."

Ironically, considering the major cultural split between Israelis and Palestinians today, it was the Arab Muslims who conquered the region in the seventh century that reopened the land to Jewish people after over five hundred years of banishment.

For the next thousand years, the region was regularly fought over along religious lines. The Palestinian region was home to Jerusalem, considered a major holy site by the Jewish, Christian, and Muslim faiths. In addition to being the site of the Temple of Solomon, the ancient Jewish King, it was also home to the Dome on the Rock (*Qubbat al-Sakhrah*), a shrine sacred to Muslims. The city is also considered holy to Christians because of the time Jesus Christ spent there. During the medieval era, the Holy Roman Empire waged several campaigns to reclaim Jerusalem from the Islamic Saracens, the Muslim people who lived there, but did not succeed.

During the late nineteenth century, rising **anti-Semitism** in Eastern Europe led to a movement called **Zionism**, which advocated for the creation of a Jewish state. European Jews began to emigrate to Palestine starting in 1880. By the outbreak

"May his bones be crushed": The Emperor Hadrian began the conflict between Israel and Palestine that continues today.

of World War I in 1914, the Jewish population of Palestine had more than tripled.

Following the war, Britain took control of Palestine in order to maintain influence over the shipping routes that ran through the Suez Canal. Rather than side with either the Arab or Jewish populations, Britain granted both communities the right of self-government. The two cultures were under great tension, each feeling they had a right to the land. By the late thirties, the British government had been unable to find a resolution to the conflict, and restricted Jewish immigration.

Never Again, but Again and Again

Under Adolf Hitler's Nazi Party, genocide against Jewish people was carried out in Germany during World War II. Over six million European Jews from Germany and other countries died during this campaign, which is now called the Holocaust, or the Shoah in Hebrew. For those who survived, either by enduring the concentration and death camps or escaping the country, there was nowhere to go. Many of them did not want to return to a country that had tried to kill them, and because of Britain's restrictions on Jews moving to Palestine, they could not go there. This angered many Palestinian Jews, who protested and petitioned the government. Unable to resolve the matter themselves, the British government appealed to the United Nations, a newly formed organization of different countries. The UN decided to divide the land into the divided territories of Palestine, which was split into two separate sections, and the state of Israel, which was officially completed in 1948.

Today, the divided Palestinian Territories are under the military control of Israel. To the east is the West Bank, which borders the Jordan River and is otherwise surrounded by Israel. The largest of the two territories, it is approximately eighty miles long and twenty-five to forty miles wide. The Gaza Strip is the territory to the west, and it shares a border with Egypt. Though the smaller of the two, at twenty-five miles long by four to seven miles wide, it does have access to the Mediterranean. Between the two of them, the West Bank has better conditions for farming, but both regions and Israel have limited access to fresh water. In 1994, Israel erected a concrete wall along 37 miles (60 kilometers) of the Gaza/Israel border, and began construction of a second wall bordering the West Bank territory. In many areas, because of conflicts between architecture and landscape, the wall actually places Palestinian land on the Israeli side of the wall.

... But Not a Drop to Drink

Because of its desert climate, water is very scarce in Israel. Since 1970, Israel has used **desalination** technology to remove the salt from seawater so it can be used for drinking and farming. Today, more than a quarter of Israel's water is produced by this method.

The first desalination plant was built in Eliat, where water was taken from the Red Sea and frozen so that the salt could be taken out. Better methods have been developed since. Following terrible droughts in the 1990s, the government constructed five new plants along the Mediterranean coast that use two different methods. One is called thermal desalination, in which the water

is boiled so that it evaporates into salt-free vapor, which can then be condensed back into liquid.

The other method is called membrane desalination. Seawater is taken in and put through several systems of cleaning. First, sea life such as jellyfish and algae are removed. Then pollutants and pathogens are cleaned out. Finally, the water is forced at a high pressure through filters made of thin plastic membranes wrapped around a tube designed to collect clean water. The remaining salt is diluted and returned to the sea. The desalinated water then has calcium added before being put through water pipes into people's homes and businesses.

Although this has improved Israel's water situation, conservation is still important, and most people only use water for necessities, rather than watering their lawns or filling swimming pools.

More from Less

While Israeli scientists are working on ways to make more water available for growing food, Palestinian agricultural engineers have begun to explore new ways to use limited water more efficiently. One type of farming that has grown in use is called **permaculture**, a system of designing landscapes that produce food while conserving resources.

There are a number of environmental factors that affect how plants can be grown. Fresh water from rainfall or irrigation is essential. Animals and insects affect farming in both good and bad ways. Seeds that have to be planted close to the surface of the soil

Olives are one of the many crops that can be grown with permaculture in Palestine.

are at risk of being eaten by birds, but those same birds can also eat insects that damage grown plants. Not all insects are harmful, though; bees are very important to farmers because they help to pollinate plants. Around the world, the bee population has been at risk because of chemical insecticides used by farmers to kill harmful insects that eat plants, like locusts and aphids. Leaving the birds to eat those bad bugs is one solution, but it does mean that farmers may have to plant more seeds to account for the birds eating some of them.

Growing plants for food can be complicated, but the secret to permaculture is that plants grow everywhere. They grow in forests, in plains, in swampland, in the sea, on mountains, in the desert, under glaciers, in caves; they even grow in smog-choked,

asphalt-paved cities. Delicate flowers can crack concrete sidewalk tiles. Permaculture is a way of agriculture that works by taking advantage of the natural behavior of plants, rather than by making plants fit into an artificial form.

Holy Text, Sacred Speech

The official language of Israel is Hebrew, a language dating back at least three thousand years. It uses twenty-two characters and, like Arabic, it is written from right to left. Arabic and Hebrew are very similar and belong to the Semitic language family.

Hebrew's role in Jewish life is also similar to Arabic's role in Muslim life. Hebrew is considered sacred in Jewish tradition, and reading and understanding the language is key to the religion itself. As part of the bar mitzvah or bat mitzvah ceremonies, in which Jewish boys and girls are recognized as adults within the community, children recite from the holy scriptures of the Torah in Hebrew, which they study as part of their religious education.

The original Hebrew language fell out of common usage in the fourth century CE as Jewish people integrated into other cultures. It survived as a written language for religious purposes and was revived in the late nineteenth and early twentieth century in the Zionist movement. For some, the decision to adopt Hebrew as a common language for Palestinian Jews seeking to create a national state was controversial. According to them, Hebrew was a holy language, and not to be used for discussing everyday matters. Another language considered was Yiddish, a pidgin language that had developed in Europe, combining parts of the Hebrew language with European words.

Dancing in the Dust

Long ago in the mountainous lands of the Levant region, people's homes were built of stone with roofs made from branches and grasses packed with dried mud. When the seasons changed, the weather would cause the packed dirt to crack and shift. It became a tradition for the people to help each other out by stomping on one another's roofs to flatten and settle the dusty mud. Over time, these movements became synced with the rhythms of Arab folk songs and moved off the roof down to the ground. The *dabke* was born.

The *dabke* connects Palestinians to their communities.

Though the dance is performed throughout the Levant region, the dabke is most popular among Lebanese and Palestinians, who consider it their national dance. It is very difficult to learn, as it contains many complex "jumps," similar to tap dancing, and requires lots of stamina to perform.

A group of *raqqasa* (female dancers) and *raqqas* (male dancers) will perform the dance in a circle. One especially skilled dancer, called the *lawweeh,* will act as a leader during the performance. From them the group will take the pace and movements of the dabke.

There are several different forms of dabke practiced today. Usually, people organize the dance into two versions: the traditional dance is performed by either only women or only men; the modern dance, however, can have both genders performing together.

The dabke has been taught within families throughout the Levant region for hundreds of generations, but at its heart it is about reaching out to connect with others. Although it will be performed with some slight variations from one country to the next, it remains an art form that celebrates community and togetherness.

Jordan

The Hashemites are a significant family in the history of the Middle East. Their roots have been traced back to Muhammad, and during World War I, they sided with the British against the Ottoman Empire. Because of this, when the British began to restructure the region, they appointed the family as rulers of Iraq, Hejaz, and Jordan. The Iraqi throne was overturned in 1958, and Hejaz was absorbed into Saudi Arabia in 1958, making Jordan the only remaining Hashemite kingdom.

In 2015, the kingdom began to use wind farms to help reduce their dependence on fossil fuels. A wind farm uses a group of turbines to generate electricity. When wind blows over the blades of the turbines, it causes them to spin, and that motion causes electrical energy to be generated. The farms were built near the mountains to take advantage of the seven miles-per-second average wind speeds there.

In addition to its focus on technology, Jordan is also an important artistic hub in the Middle East. Traditional glassblowing is an art that has made a major comeback in Jordan. Following the war between Jordan and Israel in 1967, many Palestinians emigrated from the West Bank to the city of Amman. Many glassblowers were among them, and this led to a revival in the art form. Glassblowing dates back to before the current era and involves the technique of inflating molten glass by blowing air into it. In that heated state, the glass is malleable enough to stretch, but strong enough to hold the air in. As it cools, the glass will be shaped. Glassblowing can be used to make containers and decorative works such as sculpture and beads for jewelry.

Art like glassblowing grows and changes when artists from different cultures interact.

In 1981, Queen Noor, wife of Jordan's King Abdullah II, founded the Jerash Festival of Culture and Arts, which is held in the city's ancient Roman amphitheaters. Plays written, directed, and starring Jordanians are performed every summer to an audience of 150,000 people. In addition to local theater, performing artists from other countries are invited to display their music, dance, and theater arts.

Lebanon

Geographically, Lebanon is unique among countries of the Levant region in that it has no desert or any oil reserves, and instead is lush with forests of cedar trees. Between the forests, the Mediterranean coast, and the mountains, Lebanon has pleasant weather and diverse wildlife. Unfortunately, the country has experienced many military conflicts, including a violent civil war from 1975 to 1990.

Palestinian refugees began fleeing into Lebanon following the Six-Day War with Israel in the late 1960s. By the mid 1970s, the predominantly Christian nation had a large population of Muslim refugees, paralleling Jewish immigration into Islamic Palestine earlier in the century.

Lebanon has a rich contemporary publishing culture, with over six hundred publishers producing three thousand new books every year. Although a small country, it produces 80 percent of the Arabic language books published in the Middle East. Books on Islamic topics are the country's bestsellers, closely followed by original Arabic novels. Foreign novels in translation are growing in popularity, primarily with works originally written for English-language audiences.

Khalil Gibran

One of the best-selling poets of all time, and the most famous Middle Eastern author in the English language world, Gibran was born in the Lebanese town of Bsharri in 1885. Growing up poor, he had no formal education but learned to read from Catholic priests who traveled through the area. After his father was arrested for embezzlement, his mother took him and his siblings to America in 1895, where they joined his uncle in Boston. In his early adulthood, he returned to Lebanon to immerse himself in his heritage. After studying at college, he moved back to Boston, then spent some time in Paris, France. His most famous work is *The Prophet*, first published in America in 1923. Considered one of the first novels of inspirational fiction, it concerns a prophet who has lived as an immigrant for over a decade; he tries to return home but is often waylaid by discussions about the human condition. Only a little over a hundred pages, it has sold well over nine million copies and is immensely popular in the West.

Syria

Between 2011 and 2012, Syria became a dangerous place to live due to the civil war that began from Arab Spring protests, which occurred as people revolted against their governments across the Middle East. Since then, approximately twelve million people have lost their homes due to the conflict between the military and insurgents who want to overturn President Bashar al-Assad. Extensive bombing campaigns have destroyed schools and resources. Many have been forced to flee to neighboring countries.

Materials such as mother-of-pearl are laid into wood to create *intarsia* mosaics.

While Syria is often in the news for this devastating conflict, it has also long been known as a cultural and artistic mecca in the Middle East. Seven centuries ago, Syria was known for its fine metalwork. Between the thirteenth and sixteenth centuries, handmade boxes, candlesticks, and plates made by Syrian metalworkers became very popular in Europe. One of the furniture arts that Syria became known for is intarsia. Intarsia is a form of

decorative woodworking in which an inlaid mosaic of materials such as bone and mother-of-pearl are set into treated wood. The mosaic patterns are most often geometrical, sometimes with inlaid calligraphic inscriptions as well.

Intarsia came to Syria from Egypt, and the Syrian style came to be one of the most recognized and acclaimed, even today. Intarsia furniture models that were influenced by European styles came into fashion in the 1700s. These included chests of drawers, large armchairs, sideboards, and folding screens.

Crushed into a fine powder and mixed with liquid, henna leaves become complex and beautiful body art.

4

Art, Technology, and Language in North Africa

The countries along the Mediterranean coast of the African continent are considered part of the Middle East due to the influence of Arab culture from the eighth century on. Like countries in the Levant, North African countries have a shared history with southern Europe, as well as with the African countries they border to the south. North Africa is a rich and complex cultural region where indigenous, Arab, African, and European influences all intermingle to form distinct national cultures.

Algeria

The largest of the North African countries, Algeria was predominantly populated by Berber nomads until the Arab conquests. In 1830, the French invaded Algeria, officially claiming it as a French colony in 1848. The last attempted revolt during the invasion was led by Abd al-Qadir, who is still revered as a hero by Algerians today.

During World War II, Nazi Germany invaded France and established a puppet government made up of French collaborators and sympathizers that was based in the French city of Vichy. The government in exile, headed by President Charles de Gaulle, and individuals who rejected the occupation were known as Free France. Algeria remained under the authority of Vichy France until 1942, when British, American, and Free French troops liberated the country from Vichy and Germany. However, the country had not been liberated from French rule, and still fought for independence under the restored government. In 1954, the Algerian National Liberation Front began the Algerian Revolution, which finally ended in 1962 with France conceding Algeria's independence.

At the time of the revolution, many writers from Algeria came to international fame, especially for their work criticizing French colonial rule in their country.

Mohammad Dib

Mohammad Dib was a poet and journalist who joined the Algerian Communist Party before the revolution broke out. The novels he wrote during the revolution became very popular in other countries

and showed people what life was like under French colonial rule. The authorities expelled him from the country because of his political views, as they had many other intellectuals and activists. However, while many Algerians in exile settled in Cairo, Dib chose to live in France with his French wife. Many writers who supported him appealed to the government, and he was allowed to stay.

Albert Camus

One of the writers who supported Dib was the author and philosopher Albert Camus, best known for his novel *The Stranger*. Born in Algeria in 1913 to French and Spanish parents, he was raised poor after his father died in the First World War. He studied at the University of Algiers and moved to France before the German invasion, where he wrote for various newspapers and joined the French resistance. During the revolution, he visited Algeria in an attempt to gather support for a truce. Camus was a pacifist and, while he was sympathetic to the Algerians' cause, he did not believe in the war. Many other intellectuals considered his position on the revolution to be selfish; Camus's family were European immigrants to Algeria, and some said he opposed the violence of the Algerian resistors out of concern for his mother, who still lived in Algiers. When he arrived, he was met by thousands of people shouting, "Death to Camus!" Fearing for his family and believing he could not affect any positive outcome, he stopped publicly addressing the revolution. He continued to be an important intellectual and political figure and won the Nobel Prize in 1957.

Frantz Fanon

Born in the French colony of Martinique in the Caribbean, Fanon was also an immigrant to Algeria, but unlike Camus he took a very different view of **colonialism**. After studying psychology in France, he wrote his first book, *Black Skin, White Masks*, which examined the negative psychological effects of racist colonial subjugation. In 1952, he accepted a position as chief of staff for the psychiatric

Franz Fanon was a major writer in the field of postcolonial studies.

ward of an Algerian hospital. As the violence escalated between both sides, Fanon was treating both French soldiers and Algerian civilians. After two years of the revolution, Fanon realized he could not continue to aid the French. He resigned his position at the hospital to devote himself to the cause of Algerian independence with both his words and his actions—writing essays about the French oppression and working as an ambassador to Ghana for the provisional Algerian government to help supply the revolutionaries. His final work was the book *The Wretched of the Earth*, which condemned the violence of colonialism. He died of leukemia the year before Algerian independence was achieved.

Libya

The country known today as Libya is a harsh land to live in, with desert making up 90 percent of the environment. Colonized by the Italians from 1911 to 1943, Libya became an independent kingdom in 1951. Eight years later, prospectors discovered large reserves of oil in the ground, which led to major economic and political change for the country. Further change came in 1969, when a rebel group led by twenty-seven-year old Muammar Qaddafi seized the country from King Idris while the monarch was outside the country. Following the bloodless revolution, Qaddafi proclaimed the country to be the Libyan Arab Republic and himself as the Brotherly Leader and Guide of the Revolution.

Under his leadership, the country went through a number of changes. Shifting the country to a socialist economy, the new government worked to nationalize their oil industry. Oil

money was then used to fund expanded educational curriculums and social welfare programs. But Qaddafi also adopted a strict conservative enforcement of the Islamic structure of sharia law, his interpretation of which brought international criticism for his human rights violations.

The Great Man Made River

Since 1984, Libya has been working to extract a different substance from the earth: water. Called the "Great Man Made River," the project is a system of wells and pipes designed to pump freshwater out from underground deposits and carry it north for farmland irrigation. The total project is estimated to cost about $25 billion by the time it's completed. In its final form, an estimated 1.7 billion gallons (6.4 billion liters) of water will be pumped out of 1,300 wells through thousands and thousands of miles of pipes. The pipes used are large enough to drive a small truck through.

Andalusi Music

Libya has a great tradition of music. Many of the instruments that were used thousands of years ago are still being played today by Libyan musicians, along with their modern day equivalents. These instruments include the *oud*, a stringed instrument shaped like a pear, which would be played by plucking the strings over a hollow resonating chamber; the *darbuka*, a goblet-shaped drum which is held under the arm and played by tapping the fingertips and the palm of the hand against a stretched membrane; and a type of flute cut from thick grass stalks called an *al-nay*.

Called together Andalusi music, Arab music traditions vary greatly across the country. In the south, the Tuareg, Berbers who inhabit the Saharan Desert region of North Africa, use a one-stringed violin and drums for their folk music. Tuareg musicians are typically women. Nomadic tribes also have their own styles of music, one of which, called the *huda*, mimics the sound of camels walking across the desert

Morocco

Located along the northwest corner of Africa, the country of Morocco has long been one of the most international cultures of the Middle East. The Iberian Peninsula, home to both Spain and Portugal, is located just north of the country, across a narrow strait joining the Mediterranean Sea with the Atlantic Ocean. This made it easy for people from Morocco and Europe to visit each other and trade goods with each other (and also led to early European colonization in Morocco). The French established a protectorate in Morocco in 1912, allowing the country to remain technically sovereign; in reality, however, France controlled Moroccan governance. The northern city of Tangier was declared an international zone in 1923, overseen by French, British, and Spanish powers.

Although it was rejoined to Morocco in 1956 when the French protectorate ended, it retained its multicultural influences. Many artists and writers from America and England came to the city during that time including, the American authors Paul and Jane Bowles, the playwright Tennessee Williams, the poet Allen

Ginsberg, British author and essayist George Orwell, and the rock group the Rolling Stones.

The country has always been a melting pot of cultures. From the sixteenth through eighteenth centuries, Barbary pirates operated out of the Moroccan port city of Salé. Many of the pirates in their ranks were European sailors who, disillusioned with their own country's naval authority, took up offers to join the North African pirates. One such sailor was Dutch captain Jan Janszoon van Haarlem, who joined in 1618, taking the name Murat Reis the Younger. Not all Europeans came into the Barbary culture willingly, as many were abducted as slaves, some from as far away as Iceland. Having a mix of cultures resulted in several pidgin languages made by combining words from different languages, most commonly to enable trade.

The Sun Shines on Morocco's Future

Morocco has a long history of diverse language and cultures, but what it never had was oil. This had two different effects. On the one hand, it has kept Morocco free for the most part from politics and military actions pertaining to American petroleum interests, avoiding many of the forms of conflict and compromise in other countries. However, lacking any oil resources also made the country dependent on imported coal for 97 percent of its energy needs.

That has begun to change in recent years. In 2012, Morocco began construction of a huge solar energy farm. Solar energy technology uses the energy in sunlight to create electricity. The first of three planned power plants for the farm, called Noor 1, opened in 2016 near the town of Ourzazat by the edge of the

Solar energy will radically transform Morocco's future.

Sahara desert. It is one of the world's largest solar plants and is expected to massively reduce the country's carbon emissions.

When all three plants are completed by 2020, they will produce enough surplus energy to provide electricity to European countries. This will have major benefits, as solar power is effectively limitless and produces no pollution, giving Morocco an environmentally safe form of business.

The Mark of Henna

Henna paste is able to dye the skin because of an acid called lawsone.

Henna is the Persian name for a small flowering shrub found along the Mediterranean coast of North Africa. There are so many uses for it, dating back so far in history that there's no way to be sure how it first came to be used. It is taken even today as a medicine, both topically and orally, for ailments ranging from sprains and boils to headaches and ringworm. It can also dye and condition skin and hair. The Persians also used it to color the manes and hooves of their horses.

The most popular use of henna today is as a form of body art. Throughout many different cultures from Morocco to India, henna art is part of wedding rituals for women, and sometimes men. Although the different traditions will vary, it is usually done by members of the wedding party as part of the preparations right before the wedding. Dried leaves of the plant are ground up and mixed with water, until it becomes thick. This paste is then put on the skin in decorative patterns; when the paste dries, it is removed and the dye remains on the skin.

Patterns in henna body art can appear to just be pretty decorations, but they are actually important cultural symbols. As Islam spread through the North Africa and the Middle East, permanent tattoos became discouraged, but henna art was allowed to continue. However, Islam considers it disrespectful to create images of living people and animals, so people would use geometric shapes and patterns to represent elements and animals. A diamond adorned with angles and smaller diamonds coming off its sides and corners could represent a tortoise or a frog, while a shape made from parallelograms represented seeds. These animals in turn were also symbolic: for example, lizards (drawn as a cross with two horizontal bars) stood for the search for enlightenment because they spend so much time basking in the sun to stay warm.

The Berbers

The Berbers are an indigenous people who have lived in the northern region of Africa since ancient times. Today, they primarily live in Morocco, Algeria, and Libya; as well as in smaller groups in Egypt and in some western African countries. Because of limited census data, there's no exact number for how many Berbers live in the region today, but estimates range from fifteen to twenty-five million, with most found in Morocco and Algeria.

The Berber language is called Tamazight and is rarely spoken outside of the Berber communities. There are no loan words

Wheel-thrown pottery, which is created on a potter's wheel, was one of the first art forms that could be mass-produced.

borrowed from other cultures, and the Berber language has not been assimilated into any neighboring cultures' languages.

For even small villages in the deserts and mountain regions, resources of food and supplies were scarce. In the nineteenth century, Berber men would immigrate to larger cities of other cultures to find work, to be able to provide for their families and communities back home. In these cities, the men would learn the local language and customs in order to conduct business. Often, official business was conducted in Arabic or French.

Meanwhile, the women would stay home to take care of children and the elderly, becoming not only the leaders of the community but also the teachers of the culture. The women would teach what it means to be *Imazighen*, the Berber name for themselves, and pass on the songs and poems and artistic styles. The Berber language was passed on orally largely through these women.

In the cities, Berber men would also be learning different cultures and designs while adapting their own. Pottery made by Berber men would be produced in a more industrial fashion. Rather than sculpting clay pots by hand, they would use a potter's wheel. Because of the large equipment needed, the pots of the city would be make in a workshop shared with other artisans, and reflected the design of the larger culture.

Back in the village, however, a single person however would make the pots for the entire village. These pots were intended for cooking food, as opposed to the city-made pots, which were useless for cooking but better designed for containing and transporting water. As a result of this difference in where and how the pots were

made, pots made by Berber men are more reflective of the greater regional culture, including Arabic and French traditions, while pots made by Berber women represent actual Berber cultural styles.

The difficult living conditions of the Berbers, which required this split in their community, therefore produced a unique situation where Berber language and culture was able to remain intact while still benefiting from contact with outsider civilizations.

Tunisia

As the northernmost country in Africa, the Republic of Tunisia contains the eastern end of the Atlas Mountains and the northern reaches of the Sahara desert. Beyond the mountains and sand, the country has rich, fertile soil and a long Mediterranean coastline. The government is a representative democracy, with a publicly elected president. Longtime president Zine al-Abidine Ben Ali was ousted in 2011 following Arab Spring protests leading to the so-called Jasmine Revolution. In 2014, a new version of the national constitution was agreed upon. Among the points in the new document were equal rights for women, freedom of religion but with Islam as the official state religion, and amended freedoms of speech.

Originally inhabited by nomads, primarily the Berbers, Tunisia was settled and civilized by the Phoenicians in the twelfth century BCE. The city of Carthage was later founded, which became a major trading port with Europe and the center of the Carthaginian Empire, who were major rivals of Imperial Rome until their defeat in 146 BCE. From the Arabic, the Romans knew the area as *Ifriqiyya*, which would come to be used as the name for the entire

continent: Africa. The Roman occupation paved the way for eight centuries of Christianity in the region, until the Muslim conquests. After Ottoman and French Colonial rule, Tunisia finally became independent in 1957. Parliamentary elections were introduced in 2011 after the overthrow of President Zine al-Abidine.

The rocky desert landscapes are familiar to many because the country has been a location for many films. The first movie made in North Africa was the French film *Moon Over Morocco*, which was shot in Tunisia in 1919. The most famous movie to have been made there is the first Star Wars film, which was made in 1976. Tunisia stood in for the desert planet of Tatooine, home of the series' protagonist Luke Skywalker. Today, Tunisia's own filmmakers have begun to be recognized internationally, including Férid Boughedir, who has been honored at film festivals in France and Germany.

The Motion of Light in Tunisia

Before she stood behind the cameras as a filmmaker, directing the actions of others to tell a story, Raja Amari used her own body to tell stories. Growing up, her interest in dance grew from watching classic Egyptian musicals on television. This led her to study the art of belly dancing at the Conservatoire de Tunis, the famous Tunisian dance institution. But the cabaret nightclubs where belly dancing was performed were considered below the social class of her family, and despite living on the same street as one, she never attended out of social pressure. In 1995, she began studying film in Paris. Returning to Tunisia, she was able to be on location for several films, allowing her to learn firsthand from other filmmakers. Her film *Satin Rouge* (2002) brought these two worlds

together with the story of a widowed mother becoming a cabaret dancer. Amari filmed the cabaret scenes in the very club on her old street, casting many of the dancers in the film. Produced on a budget of one million dollars, the film received numerous awards at film festivals in the United States and Italy and was praised for its portrayal of contemporary life for women in Tunisia.

Walking on Art

Decorative rugs are one of the most popular Tunisian crafts. Produced mostly in the cities of Kairouan and Jerid, there are two main types produced in the region.

The first, called *mergoum*, is a woven carpet made by threading fibers through a loom. These carpets are usually less expensive, and their design draws heavily from the Berbers. Berbers have been creating these rugs for thousands of years across North Africa, using different geometric designs and colors to signify different aspects of their culture. Today, many Berbers support themselves by making and selling these rugs.

The other kind, called *zarbia* rugs, are knotted. These rugs are made of fiber strands that are placed horizontally on a loom, called warps. When the rug is completed, the warps are cut free and tied together creating fringed tassels. The *wefts* are the fibers that are passed from side to side alternately over and under the warps, thus binding them together to produce the foundation of the carpet. The fibers that are knotted horizontally through the carpet are known as the *pile* of a rug. Different colors of fiber will be arranged in patterns to create decorative designs. In the Arabic markets called **souks**, these rugs are considered more valuable.

This Tunisian weaver's *zarbia* rug will be sold in her family's shop.

Amal al-Jubouri is an Iraqi poet and social justice activist.

5

Important Figures in Art, Technology, and Language across the Middle East

Throughout the Middle East, key figures have helped shape the culture of the region through their contributions to art and technology. While there would be too many influential figures in these fields to name all of them, this chapter introduces some important figures who have made important contributions to their respective countries.

The Gulf Region

Bahrain

Born into the Bahraini royal family in 1952, Rashid bin Khalifa al-Khalifa was first exposed to the arts in high school. At the age of fourteen, he made his first oil painting: a picture of the Khamis Mosque, the first to be built in the country. He followed his passion and studied painting in college in the United Kingdom, where he learned from the history of European painters. Although he developed his technique from the styles of foreign artists, on his return to Bahrain, he applied those to express the cultural heritage and environment of Bahrain. But al-Khalifa's biggest contribution to Bahrain came in 1983 when he was named the first president of the Bahrain Arts Society, a nonprofit organization that supports and promotes the country's artists.

Iran

"I am twenty-one. I am a homosexual," are the words that open Iranian poet and activist Payam Feili's early novella *I Will Grow, I Will Bear Fruit ... Figs.* This is a dangerous statement to make in a country where homosexuality is illegal and may be punished by death, which is why the book was published in Germany.

Openness about his sexual identity was not the only controversy that put Feili at risk. Cultural and ideological restrictions in modern Iran meant that all but one of his works had to be published in other countries. When he began working with an Israeli translator to make one of his books available in Hebrew, he fell under government suspicion. Blacklisted as a possible insurgent, he lost

his job as an editor and was arrested several times. In 2014, he was imprisoned in a shipping container for a month and a half while being interrogated by government agents. When he was finally released, so was propaganda denouncing him as a spy for foreign powers. Fearing for his life, and those of his friends and family, Feili escaped to Turkey, where he met Israelis who helped him to secure a tourist visa to Israeli. Living in Tel Aviv, he came to love the culture there and began the process to seek asylum. Being public about his homosexuality in Iran was dangerous, and violence against gays and lesbians is still an issue in other parts of the Jewish state, but the poet remains brave. "I believe it is even more dangerous when people live in hiding. Through time you start lying and you become isolated in your loneliness."

Iraq

One of the most prominent literary activists in Iraq, Amal al-Jubouri was born in the capital city of Baghdad in 1967 and came of age during the invasion of Iran. She studied English literature at the University of Baghdad before going on to work in Iraqi television and opening the publishing house Al Masar. Her first collection of poetry in Arabic, *Wine from Wounds*, was published in 1986. She moved to Munich, Germany, in her thirties, where she worked on many projects that brought together German and Arabic language poets. These projects included a conference in Yemen and publishing the magazine *Diwan*, both of which focused on poetry produced in the two languages. Following the invasion of Iraq by American-led coalition forces in 2003, she returned to her homeland, where she continued to work on exploring and teaching

language and poetry, working predominantly with orphaned girls. Her first collection of poems to be translated into English, *Hagar Before the Occupation/Hagar After the Occupation*, was published in 2011. The poems were largely concerned with the impact of the American invasion, contrasting life under the regime of Saddam Hussein with conditions in the post-war occupation. The title comes from the Biblical Hagar, the wife of Abraham, whom the Arab and Bedouin people claim to be descended from.

Kuwait

Growing up, Meqdad al-Kout loved to make people laugh, and would use a home video camera to record skits to show family and friends. But while studying at Kuwait University, he collaborated on a more serious film that would change his life. With other students, al-Kout worked on a short film called "Shards of Paper" for the school's English Day at the Faculty of Arts. The somber and experimental film received a positive response, and al-Kout was inspired to pursue filmmaking. This was a difficult path to pursue, as Kuwait didn't have any kind of dedicated filmmaking community. There were no structures of support for making movies to provide funding or resources for equipment or travel, and no education to learn cinematic techniques. Because poetry and prose are so dominant in Kuwait as narrative arts, there was very little local film culture there, and al-Kout had to seek inspiration mostly from Western filmmakers. However, he does credit and acknowledge Khaled al-Siddeeq, who directed the first Kuwaiti film *Bas ya Bahar* in 1972, as an influence. When al-Kout began

as an artist, his work was based on things in his own life, but he soon began to find inspiration in other people's experiences and ideas. Though his films make much use of surreal expression and chaotic organization, it's important to him that they remain recognizably from his own culture and reflective of his home. Though he knows the films will be seen in other cultures, he chooses to have the dialogue recorded in the Kuwaiti dialect, rather than the more widespread Arabic or English. It's his belief that by using the natural local language, the work will be seen as both honest and universal. His films have been internationally acclaimed and screened for festivals in Algeria, Iraq, Tunisia, and other countries. In 2009, his film *Banana* won the Special Jury Award at the Gulf Film Festival in the United States.

Oman

One of the most accomplished contemporary Omani artists, Alia al-Farsi is strongly influenced by Sufism. Although she first came to prominence for her paintings on canvas, Alia has expanded her work to include 3D work such as sculpture and installation art, and even furniture design. Some of the materials she has incorporated into her art include recycled paper, imported textiles, antique coins, and even cinnamon sticks. Her work has been exhibited in over twenty countries around the world, including France, China, Belgium, Turkey, Germany, and many others. She has won several awards, including the grand prize at the Annual Exhibition of the Fine Arts Society and the Dr. Suad al-Sabah Award in Kuwait.

Qatar

Following its independence from Britain in 1971, the nation of Qatar has grown into a major supporter of the arts in the Middle East. With schools, museums, and festivals dedicated to modern art in all its forms, Qatar is one of the most culturally diverse countries in the region, and much of that is owed to the artist and educator Yousef Ahmad.

Born in Doha, Qatar, in 1955, he was a part of the first generation of Qatari artists to study overseas. After earning an art and education degree in Cairo, Egypt, he returned to Qatar to work in the Ministry of Education while developing his own art style. Beginning with the traditional art of Arabic calligraphy, Ahmad began experimenting with the form, using familiar forms and existing techniques to move into more abstract images that were no longer representational of the language. His first solo exhibition was held in 1977 at the national museum, shortly after he helped to form The Three Friends, one of the first art groups that began to appear in the newly independent country. As the Qatari art scene began to flourish, Ahmad became concerned by the lack of relevant criticism and discussion. Inspired by his own ongoing research, he published *Contemporary Fine Arts in Qatar* in 1986. The book profiled many of the contemporary artists in Qatar and also recognized the organizations and institutions that were helping to support the arts. Representing his local culture is important to Ahmad, and one of the ways he explores this in his art is by using local materials; his paper comes from the indigenous palm trees, and he uses pigments made from naturally occurring minerals in the Qatar soil.

Saudi Arabia

Saudi Arabian women have been at the forefront of a recent burgeoning arts scene across their country. Much of their artwork is political and feminist in nature, using art as a form to express a political voice that has long been silenced in the country. One of the central figures of this new art scene is Manal al-Dowayan. Born in 1973, al-Dowayan first worked as a creative director in an oil company. In 2010, she became a full-time artist, eventually

Manal al-Dowayan's *Suspended Together* is an example of installation art, multidimensional artwork designed to transform a space.

becoming a leading activist for the arts in Saudi Arabia. Her works have been exhibited around the world. One of her most famous works is *Suspended Together*, a piece that features doves made from recycled permission slips that Saudi women need to have their husbands or male guardians sign in order to travel.

United Arab Emirates

Sometimes an advantage of privilege can work against you, if what you want goes outside that privilege. The daughter of the emir of Ras al-Khaimah in the United Arab Emirates, Fatima al-Qassimi was born into royalty, but her interests lay elsewhere. "Being a woman and a member of the royal family," she said in an interview, "it was hard to convince people in the fashion business that I was serious and committed to my work." As a child, she had a passion for gemology and collected decorative stones. These interests led her into making her own jewelry, starting off doing freelance design work in 2007. Three years later, she founded the brand Sough, from an old Arabic word meaning "gold." Many of her designs involved integrating the calligraphic style of the Arabic language. One of her collections, "Dubai Love," was inspired by her strong feelings for the city of Dubai and took the form of eight bracelets inscribed with different words to describe her love for the city. In the spring of 2015, she expanded into fashion with her clothing label Distinctive, featuring jalabiyas and abayas decorated with jewel embellishments and calligraphy designs. Although she has faced difficulties in being accepted as an artist, she sees these as challenges important to growth. "The roads are not always paved and easy," she advises

beginning artists, "but nothing is impossible. Put love into your work and with passion you will be able to succeed."

Yemen

The Yemeni Minister of Culture, Arwa Othman, owes her career to her teenage hobby of shopping at the marketplace. Not having a lot of money, she was looking for small, affordable items, but

The Palace of the Imam in Sana'a, Yemen, is a fine example of traditional Yemeni architecture.

grew to be very interested in many of the antiques and handcrafted art objects she found. In 2004, she founded Traditional Heritage House in Sana'a to display and preserve indigenous Yemeni arts and crafts. Some of the organization's exhibits include traditional costumes, hand-tooled leather objects, jewelry, and antique furniture. Books and photographs are also on display, making the center a resource for studying the history of Yemen. The institute was forced to close in 2011 because of political unrest and reopened a few years later, only to be robbed in 2014. But Othman is dedicated to the preservation of Yemeni culture and continues to fight for the museum's support.

The Levant Region

Egypt

Considered to be the father of modern Egyptian drama, Tawfiq al-Hakim wrote over fifty plays in his lifetime in a range of styles and themes. Born in 1898, in Alexandria, he wrote his first play at the age of nineteen. However, his family discouraged him from pursuing the arts, and he hid his involvement with the theater from his parents. To appease them, he went to France to study law. He returned to Egypt, where he worked as a circuit judge, but he continued his interest in theater and writing. Working in the Egyptian courts inspired him to write his first novel, *The Maze of Justice*. The book was successful enough to allow him to resign from his job and devote himself to writing. His work for the stage was very popular, because it covered a range of themes and styles. Some of the things he wrote about often were life in the modern

Egyptian playwright Tawfiq al-Hakim explored the Arabic language with his contemporary plays.

world of industrialization and international relations, the problems of government and politics, and conflicts between spirituality and the material world. One project that he was unable to complete was to create a form of Arabic for use in the theater. This "third language" would have combined the Arabic of classical literature with modern colloquial forms that had been common in modern Egyptian theater. It was al-Hakim's hope that such a form of language would have made plays accessible as both performative works, as well as literature to be read as a text.

Israel

Today, one of Israel's leading industrial fields is the manufacturing of chemicals, and the woman who helped make that happen was Dahlia Greidinger. A fifth-generation Palestinian Jew, she was born in Tel-Aviv in 1926. Growing up, she attended a private Hebrew school in Haifa, which had opened the year before the outbreak of World War One. After the Second World War, she left her homeland to study chemistry in Switzerland, where she earned a master's degree in science with distinction. After returning home to the newly formed state of Israel, she began to both teach and do research at the Israel Institute of Technology, where she would earn a doctorate in 1958. After completing her terminal degree, she found work at Deshanim Fertilizers & Chemicals Ltd. Ten years later, she was appointed to the board of directors and made Director of Research and Development. Recognized and respected for her work as a senior scientist, Greidinger was instrumental in the development of Israel's chemical industry. She developed innovative fertilization systems, registered many patents, and

published a large number of scientific papers. Her contributions to the field of chemistry are honored with the Dahlia Greidinger Fertilizer Research Fund, established by her surviving family.

Jordan

With a PhD in molecular biology, Dr. Rana Dajani has consulted for the Higher Council for Science and Technology in Jordan, written for the magazines *Science* and *Nature*, and served on the United Nations' Women Civil Society Advisory Group. It's in front of a classroom of developing students that she feels she does her most important work, however. "I teach evolution to university students in Jordan," she writes in an essay for *Nature*. "Almost all of them are hostile to the idea at first." But she goes on to say that by asking her students to undertake challenging ideas in the classroom, they can bring that same level of questioning to other areas of their lives. In 2014, she was named one of the most influential scientists in the Islamic World and one of the most powerful women in the Arabic world.

Lebanon

When the Lebanese civil war broke out in 1975, the Beirut-born artist Mona Hatoum was visiting London, England; she was unable to return home. For the next several years, she enrolled in British art schools and became a performance artist, someone whose art involves public action before an audience but is not in the traditional form of musical or theatrical presentation. She carried over some of these techniques and ideas into her later work in sculpture and installation art, creating pieces that took up whole

rooms and used elements of video and photography to involve the audience. Her work, which explores ideas about violence, gender identity, and body politics, has been exhibited in galleries and museums around the world.

Palestine

Murad Al Khuffash is a Palestinian farmer who has worked for decades to help develop means of sustainable farming for people in the West Bank. In 2006, he helped establish a permaculture farm in Marda that provides both food and education, teaching people how to grow food more efficiently in inhospitable environments and limited spaces. Agricultural self-sufficiency for Palestine is Al Khuffash's main goal. His home farm, a mere half-acre, has been repurposed to not only provide food for his family but to also offer instruction to other people looking to create their own gardens. For the future, he plans to expand on Palestinian self-sufficiency beyond fruits and vegetables to include urban livestock and alternative energy, to make the occupied territories as independent from Israel as possible.

Syria

"In my films, I invite people to be consciously open to listening and seeing," wrote the Syrian filmmaker Diana el Jeiroudi in an artist's statement for a showing in New York. "I think those are the human skills that we need to value most." Born in Damascus in 1977, she began working in the field of documentary film in 2002.

Producing, distributing, and promoting films, she confounded the Proaction Film company with other documentary filmmakers. Her first film, *The Pot*, was a short work released in 2005 that explored issues about pregnancy and women's relationships with their bodies. A few years later, she wrote, directed, and produced the film *Dolls: A Woman From Damascus*, which wove together interviews with a Damascene housewife and the marketing executive behind Barbie-style dolls marketed to Arab girls.

North Africa

Algeria

Born Fatima-Zohra Imalayen in 1936, to a Muslim family, Assia Djebar was raised in a small seaport town on the coast of Algeria. Growing up, she attended a Quranic private school where she was one of only two girls. She went on to public education in Algiers, where she was the only Muslim in her class. In 1957, she published her first novel, *The Thirst*. Fearing her father's disapproval, she had it published under the pen name Assia Djebar. Her novels and poems addressed the struggles of being a feminist intellectual living under colonialism. After independence, other Algerian intellectuals criticized her for still writing in French, which was seen as a language of oppression. Sympathetic to this idea, she would incorporate both French and Arabic linguistics in her later novels. In 2005, Djebar was the first Algerian and only the fifth woman to be accepted into the French Academy, an important French cultural council.

Libya

Growing up as a teenager in the 1960s, Ahmed Fakroun was fascinated with the rhythms and harmonies of Western pop music, leading him to pick up the electric bass as his first instrument. This led him then to the piano and harmonica, and eventually traditional Arabic instruments like the mandola, ud, and saz. Blending together his love of pop music with traditional Libyan sounds and songs, he became a pioneer of Arabic world music, bringing together international influences and reinterpreting them to create a modern style of Arabic music. Popular in his own country, he has also performed and recorded internationally with many record labels and performance venues.

Morocco

Dr. Ismahane Elouafi is a woman of strong beliefs. A scientist, geneticist and environmentalist, she believes that, in order to alleviate discrimination and poverty, science should be at the heart of all forms of development planning. After earning her PhD in genetics from Cordoba University in Spain, the Moroccan scientist and environmentalist became Director General for the UAE-based International Centre for Biosaline Agriculture in 2012. The Centre focuses on research and development for irrigation, desalination, and other agricultural technologies. Under her leadership, the organization has begun to examine the connections between income and nutrition.

Tunisia

The first Tunisian women's magazine was founded in 1959 by Safia Farhat. Before becoming a feminist publisher, she studied at the Tunis Institute of Fine Arts, where she later became director in 1966. In addition to overseeing the school, she also headed its new school of architecture. During her lifetime, she also designed postage stamps and helped found the Tunisian Association of Democratic Women. She worked in many artistic mediums, including frescoes, stained glass, and fiber arts.

Chronology

8000 BCE   Earliest examples of rock art in Libya.

3000 BCE   Writing is invented in ancient Mesopotamia.

313 CE   Roman emperor Constantine legalizes Christianity.

610   Muhammad becomes founding prophet of Islam.

1095   European crusades to take Jerusalem begin.

1453   Ottomans conquer Byzantium; Constantinople is renamed Istanbul.

1830   France invades Algeria.

1914   Austrian archduke Franz Ferdinand is assassinated and World War I begins.

1930s   Oil is discovered in several Middle Eastern nations and regions.

1939	Germany invades Poland, and World War II begins.
1948	The State of Israel is founded.
1979	Iran is declared an Islamic republic following a revolution.
1990	Iraq invade Kuwait, which begins the Gulf War.
2003	US-led invasion of Iraq begins.
2011	Arab Spring protests begin.

Map of the Region

Art, Technology, and Language across the Middle East

Glossary

anti-Semitism Originally meaning racism against the different Semitic people, it now refers specifically to prejudice and/or hatred of Jewish people.

Bedouins Nomadic people of the deserts of North Africa and the Middle East.

Caliph A spiritual leader in Islam who claims to be descended from the Prophet Muhammad.

colonialism The practice of one country economically exploiting another country by occupying it and gaining partial or complete political control of the government.

desalination A process by which ocean water is made drinkable by removing the salt.

dialect A form of language that is specific to a region or cultural group.

emir A political or military leader, appointed rather than elected.

empire A group of regions or countries under one single authority.

Farsi The official language of Iran.

fiber arts Art forms that make use of material made from fibers such as wool, cotton, or grass.

Art, Technology, and Language across the Middle East

ghazal An Arabic poetic form, composed in honor of an authority figure or deity.

Hebrew The official language of Israel.

henna Persian name for a type of plant whose leaves are used for both medicinal and artistic purposes.

nomadic people A community of people without a permanent home who travel from place to place.

permaculture A system of designing landscapes that produce food while conserving resources.

pidgin language A combination of words and phrases from two different languages, usually to enable trade.

protectorate A relationship where a stronger state protects a weaker one, in exchange for some or all political powers.

souks The Arabic term for open-air markets.

Sufism Mystical interpretation of Islam.

Zionism The political movement to create a Jewish state.

Further Information

Books

Al-Khalili, Jim. *The House of Wisdom: How Arabic Science Saved Ancient Knowledge and Gave Us the Renaissance.* New York: Penguin Press, 2011.

Brodsky, Judith K., and Ferris Olin. *The Fertile Crescent: Gender, Art, and Society.* Concord, NH: Rutgers University Institute for Women and Art, 2012.

Kennedy, Hugh. *The Great Arab Conquests: How the Spread of Islam Changed the World We Live In.* Philadelphia, PA: Da Capo Press, 2007.

Naylor, Philip C. *North Africa, Revised Edition: A History from Antiquity to the Present.* Austin, TX: University of Texas Press, 2015

Pappé, Ilan. *The Modern Middle East: Asocial and Cultural History.* New York: Routledge, 2014.

Websites

Arabic Without Walls

http://arabicwithoutwalls.ucdavis.edu/aww

This website, hosted by the University of California Davis's language department, has useful information on the history of the Arabic language.

The Museum of Science and Technology in Islam

http://museum.kaust.edu.sa

Located in Saudi Arabia, this museum showcases the history of science and technology in the Middle East.

Smithsonian National Museum of African Art

http://africa.si.edu

This website highlights the Smithsonian Institute's collection of art from the continent of Africa, including North African works of art.

Bibliography

Al-Khalili, Jim. *The House of Wisdom: How Arabic Science Saved Ancient Knowledge and Gave Us the Renaissance.* New York: Penguin Press, 2011.

Alfozaie, Abdullateef. "Fatima Al-Qassimi Jewelry: Arabesque Designs and Lustrous Pearls." *Khaleeejesque,* June 6, 2009. http://www.khaleejesque.com/2009/06/fashion/fatima-al-qassimi-designs.

Banham, Martin. *A History of Theater in Africa.* Cambridge, UK: Cambridge University Press, 2004.

Brett, Michael, and Elizabeth Fentress. *The Berbers.* Cambridge, MA: Blackwell Publishers, 1996.

Brodsky, Judith K., and Ferris Olin. *The Fertile Crescent: Gender, Art, and Society.* Concord, NH: Rutgers University Institute for Women and Art, 2012.

East, Ben. "Emirati Author Mohammed Al Murr speaks to new opportunity for UAE writers." *The National,* April 19, 2016. http://www.thenational.ae/arts-life/books/emirati-author-mohammed-al-murr-speaks-to-new-opportunity-for-uae-writers.

Kerahner, Isabel. "Blacklisted in Iran, Gay Poet Seeks Asylum in Israel." *New York Times*, March 2, 2016. http://www.nytimes.com/2016/03/03/world/middleeast/blacklisted-in-iran-gay-poet-seeks-asylum-in-israel.html.

Mahmoud, Kassem AlSayed. "Kassem AlSayed Mahmoud." *Scholars at Risk Network*, May 5, 2015. https://www.scholarsatrisk.org/spotlight/sar-spotlight-kassem-alsayed-mahmoud.

Pappé, Ilan. *The Modern Middle East: A Social and Cultural History.* New York: Routledge, 2014.

Reidy, Eric. "Palestinian farmers hungry for change." *Aljazeera*, October 26, 2013. http://www.aljazeera.com/indepth/features/2013/10/palestinian-farmers-hungry-change-20131019131141244255.html.

Index

Page numbers in **boldface** are illustrations. Entries in **boldface** are glossary terms.

About the Author

Greg Baldino holds a Bachelor of Arts in fiction writing from Columbia College Chicago, where he studied genre literature and twentieth-century social history. Since 2007, his journalism and essays have appeared in publications including the *Los Angeles Review of Books*, *Remedy Quarterly*, and *The Writer*. With artist Noelle Blanc, he produced the graphic essay "Blumenkraft" for the comics anthology *War: The Human Cost*. His essay "A Better Class of Criminal" was translated for the Spanish anthology *Batman Desde La Pereferia*. He lives in Chicago in a house made of books with an ambiguous number of cats.

W9-CFB-419